AFFIRMATION JOURNAL FOR POSITIVE THINKING

AFFIRMATION JOURNAL FOR POSITIVE THINKING

Prompts and Inspiration to Help You
Harness Peace and Joy

KELLY SWANSON

ROCKRIDGE
PRESS

For general information on our other products and services or to obtain technical support, please contact our Customer Care Department within the United States at (866) 744-2665, or outside the United States at (510) 253-0500.

Rockridge Press publishes its books in a variety of electronic and print formats. Some content that appears in print may not be available in electronic books, and vice versa.

TRADEMARKS: Rockridge Press and the Rockridge Press logo are trademarks or registered trademarks of Callisto Media Inc. and/or its affiliates, in the United States and other countries, and may not be used without written permission. All other trademarks are the property of their respective owners. Rockridge Press is not associated with any product or vendor mentioned in this book.

Interior and Cover Designer: Karmen Lizzul
Art Producer: Samantha Ulban
Editor: Sean Newcott
Production Editor: Jael Fogle
Production Manager: Martin Worthington

Author photo courtesy of Sarah Petty Photography

Paperback ISBN: 978-1-63807-297-3
R0

THIS JOURNAL BELONGS TO

_____

Introduction

IF YOU ARE HERE, WE WERE DESTINED TO meet, and I have a message meant for you. So listen closely: I have spent most of my life as a motivational speaker and comedian, which means I will tell you that you can do anything and then I will tell you I'm just kidding. Did you laugh? Good. There are more smiles waiting for you inside.

I don't just come to you as someone with lots of experience with positive thinking. I come to you as someone whose life was saved by affirmations. When I was young, I believed in the fairy tales that promised me a charmed life, a loving prince, a big castle, and a happily-ever-after. I spent my life trying to measure up to that myth. Know the feeling?

For the longest time, I thought that fate was in control of my story. But life doesn't work that way. We can't control the story—or can we? I remember the exact moment my life changed. My heart was broken, and I was wallowing in heartbreak when I felt a moving message downloading itself into my deepest depths. Where were the words coming from? Did I read them somewhere? Were they stitched on a pillow at my grandmother's house? Had I seen them on a refrigerator magnet? Something perhaps penned by the famous poet Anon?

The message's origin didn't matter, because I heard the positive affirmation so clearly: *You can't change what just happened, but you can change what happens next.* In that moment, I realized I couldn't control what life gave me, but I *could* control the story I wrote with what life gave me. And so I did. How? By changing my inner script:

what I believed about myself, my worth, my abilities, and how I wanted my life to look on my own terms. Here's the really cool part: The more I wrote about the life I wanted, the more it came to be!

That has become the core foundation of what I teach—the idea that getting the life you want starts with creating the mindset that works for you instead of against you. My philosophy is that the positive affirmations you feed yourself daily will guide how you see yourself, your world, and the situations you face in a positive way. These teachings are also based on my core belief that what we focus on becomes what we receive.

You may be nodding wildly because you get it, or maybe you're thinking that this is too good to be true. Or perhaps you're somewhere in the middle. Whatever you may be thinking, whatever might have brought you to this journal, there is something here for you. We just need to equip you with the right tools and mindset to write, or rewrite, your story.

My hope is that this journal will be your source for inspiration and guidance and that it will be just what you need to fall in love with yourself, either for the first time or all over again. My goal is to help you write an affirming and positive story that works *for* you. Welcome to the place where our hearts meet. Grab my hand, take a deep breath, and let's jump in! Your happily-ever-after is waiting.

How to Use This Journal

THIS JOURNAL IS DESIGNED FOR YOU TO USE when you need it and when it fits your schedule. You don't have to go through the book in order. Just flip through and choose an affirmation that fits your mood or current situation. This resource is based on the belief that most of us are more likely to create positive change when we break down our actions into workable, bite-size steps. This gives you time to really digest the information and put it into practice—one affirmation at a time.

Each of the 40 unique sections in this journal includes an affirmation, a guided journal prompt, affirmation guidance, and "Embrace Positivity", a fact or practice that concludes the section.

Each **affirmation** is a short positive statement you can incorporate into your life and adopt as one of your core beliefs. They focus on a specific thought or belief necessary for self-growth and empowerment. Think of the affirmation as a mantra you can repeat to yourself regularly.

Following the affirmation is a **guided journal prompt** that helps you reflect on the affirmation. Through the prompt, you will discover how this particular affirmation applies to your life. This step heightens your sense of self-awareness as you detect where the true issues lie. Writing your thoughts down is a critical stage of the process. Don't skip this part. It will be very powerful and enlightening. The act of writing down your reflections will serve you in a big way.

The **affirmation guidance** is intended to guide you in the process of taking what you have explored so far and creating your own positive affirmation, customized to your life and circumstances. You're literally rewriting your inner script. These positive affirmations are crafted to speak to your own life and will be the true key in changing the way you think.

The **Embrace Positivity** entry shares some simple practices or tips to help you embrace this new affirmation and incorporate it in a lasting way. Action helps empower a new mindset in that it forces you to start walking your talk (or should I say "walking your thought"?). This is the part where you put your new mindset into action.

Don't worry about whether you are doing this journal "right." The main point is that you're steering yourself toward a mentality that is positive and supports a peaceful, abundant life. And if you make the effort, I assure you that you will be rewarded.

I hold the pen. This story is *mine*. I'm filling my inner script with *good* things because I deserve it.

Hello, my friend. It's time to check in on that inner script. What have your inner thoughts been telling you lately? Were they kind or unkind? Who's writing your story today—the good voices or the bad? It's time to find the joy killers and send them packing!

_____

_____

_____

_____

_____

_____

_____

Time to stand up to any nasty little voices in your head and put them in their place! Here's a little help to get you started:

One of the negative voices is telling me I am _____

_____.

But this is a lie.

The truth is _____

_____

_____

_____

_____

_____.

And here's why: _____

_____

_____

_____

_____

EMBRACE POSITIVITY

Look at your bold self, standing up to that nasty little inner voice! It will keep buzzing around you like a honeybee on a blooming flower. Mine did, and it kept telling me I didn't deserve my own success. Even though I knew it was wrong, I still worried about it—because *saying* isn't the same as *believing*. That takes practice. So do what I did:

Get a small notebook and a pencil. Tie a piece of string around your wrist or a finger (not too tight!). Let this be a reminder that whenever you hear that negative belief in your head, pause, recite the positive affirmation, and mark in your notebook that you had that negative thought. Repeat the process until you don't hear that negative thought anymore. Before you know it, those pesky thoughts won't be buzzing in the way of your positive self-talk!

Today I choose *contentment*. I stand in the *joy* of knowing I have everything I need. I am enough.

Are you living in the land of "if only"—thinking that if only you had this, you would be happy? What is on your "if only" list? If you get these things, what will that feel like? Could you have that same feeling right now? Can you find peace without these things?

_____

_____

_____

_____

_____

_____

_____

It's okay to want more from life, but don't put your happiness on hold while you pursue it. The "if only" isn't your key to peace. *You* are. Write an affirming statement that reminds you that you're at peace where you are, even if you are not yet where you want to be. _____

_____

_____

_____

_____

_____

_____

_____

_____

_____

_____

_____

_____

EMBRACE POSITIVITY

When I was a child, instead of being in awe of what my family had, I couldn't help but notice what my family *didn't* have. One night, when I told my parents that I felt like we were lacking, my father said, "If you always look around at who has more, you will always come up short. And you'll always be poor. If you look around at who has less, you will always come out ahead. You will always feel rich. The luckiest are the ones who know how to turn nothing into something."

In that moment, I learned that contentment is a choice made where I start, not a result of where I land. When you create your life plan, make sure that the affirmations you tell yourself don't hang your happiness on where you land but rather on where you stand.

Today is a new day. Yesterday is gone, and I will not glance back. I move toward a fresh start.

Reflect on a challenging experience. Despite what might have been tough about this time, your life was sending you a message. Did you hear it? What was it? If it was painful, can you find the gift in it? How are you stronger now? What silver lining will you keep as a reminder of this moment in your life?

Affirmation Journal for Positive Thinking

Today I choose to turn the page on yesterday. I acknowledge that it taught me

_____

_____

_____

_____.

It was put in my life so that I would _____

_____

_____

_____.

The positive message I will take away is _____

_____

_____

_____

_____

_____

_____.

I will choose to rise up, smile again, and face a new day.

EMBRACE POSITIVITY

Sometimes it takes the dark to help us find our way to the light. While we may not understand everything that happens in our lives, especially the people or events we don't willingly invite in, we can always trust that there is something to be learned. Through every storm we weather, if we keep our eyes open, we will see the sun shining at the end.

Acknowledging that gift allows us to move forward with a sense of peace. If we focus on the positive, we will find our path to joy again. If we continue to focus on the dark clouds, we will remain in the negative. As the saying goes, "Where we look is where we land." Find a picture (or create one) that represents you looking toward the sun—toward the positive—and put it somewhere you will see it often.

Today I have a big, bold *ask*. I boldly claim my victory. It is already in motion. I am excited.

Sometimes we get discouraged because we feel like we haven't achieved our goals. But the truth is, we can't reach a goal we haven't yet defined with intention. Think about what it is that you really wish to achieve or want to come to fruition in your life. What is your most important, most exciting goal?

Today you can gain clarity on what specifically you are asking from the universe. Don't be shy. The universe is waiting to give it to you. It just doesn't know what you want yet.

Today I boldly ask for _____

_____

_____

and_____

_____

_____

_____ and _____

_____. And here is what it will look like when it

happens: _____

_____

_____

_____

_____.

EMBRACE POSITIVITY

Does it make you feel nervous to ask for something? Afraid to make a declaration? Do you feel like a big ask is selfish or "unattractive"? If so, I want you to know that big asks are incredible. The more you ask for, the more you end up with! The bigger the ask, the bigger the bottom line.

Define your big ask and put it out there in the world. A wonderful method to help you visualize what you want is storyboarding. Gather some magazines and cut out pictures that speak to the life you want to create and paste them on a board, telling a story from beginning to end. Narrate your storyboard as if it's already in motion to a close friend, a family member, or yourself. This is not the time to be humble. Your talents were given to you for a reason.

I will not let negative emotions drive my car. They are simply a "check engine" light for a faulty belief about myself.

Are you making decisions based on fact or emotion? Just because you feel it doesn't make it true. List all the emotions you have been feeling lately. When you finish, read the list and circle the negative ones. When you look at the feelings you circled, ask, "Is this really a fact? Or am I reacting to an emotion that is contrary to the fact?"

Today I feel_____

because somebody said or did _____

_____

_____.

I honor this emotion and allow myself to feel it. But this feeling is not in control

of me. It's just an indication that I have a negative belief about myself that needs

rewriting. What is that negative belief? I will rewrite it to say:

_____

_____

_____

_____

_____

_____

_____

_____

_____

_____.

EMBRACE POSITIVITY

Sometimes we doubt our own abilities. Sometimes we worry that the people around us might not want to hear what we have to say, don't care about what we think, and/or don't appreciate what we have to offer. When these negative thoughts creep in, be sure to look at the truth in front of you instead of the feeling inside of you.

I highly encourage you to put your feeling in the back seat and let truth drive. When a negative or false belief about yourself gets too noisy, think: *Just because I feel it, does it make it true? No. Truth trumps emotion. Truth drives me, not emotion. I know what is true about myself based on evidence and facts, and that is enough.*

Look out, world, here I come. And don't even try to get in my way. I am ON FIRE.

Are you celebrating and dancing today because you are so cool and awesome? If you aren't, write in your journal about what's stopping you. When you're done, have a dance party for yourself and dance to your greatness. Don't make any excuses—the world can wait for you to take the time to love yourself.

_____

_____

_____

_____

_____

_____

_____

Give yourself permission to get out there and celebrate your awesomeness!

Today I'm having a party for myself. Here is what I'm celebrating: _____

_____

_____

_____

_____.

Here is how I will celebrate: _____

_____

_____

_____

_____

_____

_____

_____

_____.

I'm awesome. That's right: I was born for GREATness.

EMBRACE POSITIVITY

Sometimes it can be hard to embrace the idea of celebrating ourselves. As children, most of us were taught that it is not polite to brag about our accomplishments and talents. But it's important to remember that bragging (being pompous, cocky, or arrogant) is not the same as joyfully celebrating all that makes you special and amazing. Life is short, and you deserve to celebrate YOU. The world cannot see how great you are if you don't see it first!

Your assignment for today is to choose something to celebrate—a new job, a completed home project, a creative endeavor, or whatever you can think of, big or small; the possibilities are endless. Now plan your celebration. Pick a date and place, invite your friends, and above all, allow yourself to celebrate YOU and be celebrated in return.

Today I take ownership of my part in this particular situation. I grow from acknowledging when I am at fault.

We often assume that we're the hero in our own story. But what if sometimes we're actually the villain? Not because we're bad, but because we're human and capable of missteps. Taking ownership of our part will help us grow. Is there a story where you might be at fault? Describe it.

Think about a situation that had negative drama for you and those involved. Now look closer to determine whether your actions or inactions might have added to the negativity. What is the possible positive impact of taking ownership of your part? Create an affirmation that describes what taking ownership looks like for you. _____

_____

_____

_____

_____

_____

_____

_____

_____

_____

_____

_____

EMBRACE POSITIVITY

The key to having the life we want is often a result of understanding how much control and responsibility we have in creating that life by taking ownership of the choices we've made, the ones we make today, and the ones we will make in the future. Forward movement past an obstacle first requires our awareness of the obstacle, our desire to move past it, and the knowledge that our decisions will direct the path.

While it may sting to realize that our choices brought us to where we are today, it is also incredibly freeing to know that our choices will be what take us to tomorrow and a more positive future. While there is so much in life that we cannot control, there is a lot in life that we *can* control. Our mindset is the most important one, as it guides our path.

Today I don't *feel* brave, but's that okay, because I *choose* to be brave. My dream is bigger than my fear.

How do you find the courage to do the things that scare you? Do you wait to take the leap until you feel brave enough? Do you see fear as something to get rid of? What do you do when you are facing something that scares you?

_____

_____

_____

_____

_____

_____

_____

This opportunity scares me, but today I choose bravery. I may not feel it, but I will choose it anyway. I have been brave before, when I _____

_____

_____

and the time I _____

_____

_____

_____

_____

_____

_____.

I will be brave again. I will jump. Because my dream is bigger than my fear and I deserve_____

_____

_____

_____

_____.

EMBRACE POSITIVITY

Because I put myself out there in my career and personal life, I'm often asked how I find the courage to deal with the fear of taking risks. The truth is that fear doesn't go away; rather, we must learn to embrace it, honor it, and boldly move through it. We can *choose to be* brave instead of *waiting to feel* brave.

You can build your bravery muscle. If you pick something small that you need to do, commit to it, and then do it, you're exercising and building your bravery muscle. Once you accomplish what you set your mind to, be sure to celebrate. Small acts of courage strengthen that bravery muscle and prepare you for when you need to be extra brave and tackle bigger obstacles. Never be afraid to choose to be brave. You will find that you achieved victory the moment you jumped into the unknown.

Today I lovingly caress my wrinkles and scars and honor them for telling the story of my life.

Do you ever avoid your own reflection? If so, why? Look at your body and describe what you see; include all the parts from head to toe. Are you judging your body by what you think it *should* look like rather than what it actually looks like?

_____

_____

_____

_____

_____

_____

_____

Affirmation Journal for Positive Thinking

One of the wonderful things about positive thinking is that we *can* change the way we see ourselves. We can write a story today that is different from yesterday's, one that celebrates us for who we are and pushes us toward the life we want to live. Write an affirmation now that honors the body you are in. _____

_____

_____

_____

_____

_____

_____

_____

_____

_____

_____

_____

EMBRACE POSITIVITY

Every single one of us is unique and different, and it is natural that sometimes those differences can infiltrate our self-confidence and make us feel like we don't fit in or don't belong. But sometimes the very secret to our success is in the way we stand out from the crowd: what sets us apart from others and allows us to authentically connect with those around us.

Don't be afraid to be yourself—people will connect with your authenticity; they will respond positively to how real you are, and they will gravitate toward what makes you relatable. Everything that makes you *you* is a testament to a life well lived. Don't focus so much on *what isn't* that you miss the beauty of *what is*.

Perfection is impossible, but my hard work matters. I will focus on delivering what I promise and be proud of that.

Are you a perfectionist? Who defines *perfection*? Do you feel like your work is never good enough? If you feel this way, who and what is it not good enough for? Are you aiming for something that is unrealistic and unattainable? Is the quest for perfection causing you to miss deadlines or not do it at all?

_____

_____

_____

_____

_____

_____

Affirmation Journal for Positive Thinking

Take a moment to reflect on what you expect from your work, whether it's professional, personal, creative, clinical, etc. Focus on what can be measured, defined, and obtained. Create a positive affirmation about meeting both your own reasonable expectations and those of your colleagues/peers. If you're unsure about what others expect, ask for their perspective. _____

_____

_____

_____

_____

_____

_____

_____

_____

_____

_____

_____

EMBRACE POSITIVITY

Are you overly focused on being perfect? Most of us can sympathize with that feeling. Many of us have also had moments where we feel so fearful of being less than perfect that we end up failing. As long as we are holding ourselves to impossible standards of perfection, we will never feel like we are good enough or that something is perfect just the way it is, imperfections and all.

A good way to reframe this kind of thinking is to ask yourself, "Did I deliver on my promise?" and "Did someone in need get what they expected?" These are goals that can be reasonably measured. Aiming for perfection can rob you of your sense of joy, and you deserve to feel joyful. So, if your answer to these questions is yes, celebrate your accomplishment.

Today I let go of making the *best* choice in how I nourish my body and focus on making the *better* choice.

Are you beating yourself up for not following your own rules when it comes to food? Is this keeping you from making good choices? Can you focus on what you are doing to nourish your body and express gratitude to yourself for making that choice? Maybe you went for a nice walk, danced to a song you love, ate something satisfying and delicious—think of how you've shown up for your body today.

Affirmation Journal for Positive Thinking

Create a new goal for your body that feels easier to reach. Maybe something like:

Today I am not going to worry about making perfect choices. I am just going to focus on making the best possible choice when it's time to feed my body. Here is what that may look like: _____

_____

_____

_____

_____

_____

_____

_____

_____

_____

_____

_____

_____.

EMBRACE POSITIVITY

It can be challenging to think about achieving our larger goals, such as always following a healthy and nourishing diet, especially when we're starting out or feeling pressured to get it right and see results immediately. Instead, think about your goal as a step-by-step process—one that doesn't have to be perfect every moment of every day, but one that embraces being the best you can be in that moment.

Whatever your ultimate goal is, put the message "Making a BETTER choice today is the best choice" on a sticky note and hang it somewhere helpful, such as in the pantry, on the refrigerator, or on a cabinet door. Let this message encourage you every day; no pressure. Just as coins add up to dollars, better choices add up, too.

My mistakes do not define me, but they do have something to teach me. I am not perfect, and that is perfectly okay.

Have you been focusing on a past mistake? Is it on a continuous loop inside your head? Is there something you have been refusing to forgive yourself for? List any mistakes or nagging thoughts that still sting a little—or a lot—and reflect on them and what they really mean to you.

_____

_____

_____

_____

_____

_____

_____

Write yourself a love note forgiving yourself for that mistake. Using positive words, remind yourself you aren't perfect, accept responsibility for your part, identify what you learned, and (here's the hard part) thank your mistake for the gift it gave you. Perhaps it's a lesson learned, a chance to make it right, a fresh start, a greater sense of self, or inner strength. _____

_____

_____

_____

_____

_____

_____

_____

_____

_____

_____

_____

EMBRACE POSITIVITY

Somewhere along the way, we've all made a mistake. Probably more than one. And sometimes BIG ones. Making mistakes is a necessary part of life. Some are accidental. Some are intentional. Some are unavoidable. But in every single one, we have a choice in what we do with that mistake. We still have a window of opportunity to turn the bad into something good.

Once the mistake is over—and it does always come to an end—you get to write the story of what you will do with it. We all know that forgiving others is a virtue, but sometimes we're not so good at forgiving ourselves—that is, until today. It's time. And remember this: You are NOT your mistake. It's something you did, not something you are.

I am loved. I am here for a purpose. I will choose that truth, even if I don't feel it.

Every single one of us serves a specific purpose. We all matter, and our existence means something. We matter not only to the world but also to the people in it. What do you believe about your existence? Where do you find your purpose?

_____

_____

_____

_____

_____

_____

_____

Imagine something you have (or had) that holds your treasures, like a chest or a hollowed-out book on a shelf. Each item inside has personal meaning, symbolizing something good in your life. Affirm that you are part of the universe's treasure chest and the good in our world, and explore what that means to you.

_____

_____

_____

_____

_____

_____

_____

_____

_____

_____

_____

EMBRACE POSITIVITY

Today you're going to bury a time capsule to serve as evidence of what life was like on the day you buried it. Your capsule should contain items that depict the good you have brought into the world. Maybe it's a painting you've done, a picture of you and a loved one, something you've written, or whatever you feel represents your contribution to the world.

This is your way of placing yourself in the treasure chest of the universe. This is a great activity for the whole family, a group of friends, or a work team, or you can do it on your own. Bury it someplace safe and decide when you will dig it up. On that date, look at the treasures in your chest. Remember, you *do* matter, you *are* loved, and you are here for a purpose—even if you can't see it yet.

My world is filled with an abundance of goodness. Today I will find that goodness and add to it.

Where are good things happening around you? Where can you look for more? How can you go out into the world and add to the goodness this week? How might focusing only on finding, doing, and receiving good affect you, your life, and the people around you?

Affirmation Journal for Positive Thinking

Create a plan for finding, doing, and receiving good this week. Consider the places you can go and the people you can see, as well as other ways to positively communicate with the world around you. Create a powerful affirmation to help you remember to do all three—find, do, and receive. _____

_____

_____

_____

_____

_____

_____

_____

_____

_____

_____

_____

EMBRACE POSITIVITY

Have you known people who are constantly angry, negative, and bitter? It is not because they got a bigger helping of negativity in their lives, but because they are *choosing* to let the negative things be their focus. Remember, what you focus on becomes what you see; it's your choice.

You certainly don't need the headaches, heartaches, and body aches that come with negative thinking. You can choose joy. You can choose laughter. You can choose love. You can choose goodness. By focusing on the positive, you surround yourself with the good things in life and pull more good into your life. Be intentional about what you seek and notice the positives in any situation.

Today I step into my full power as a leader, knowing that I have been called for this purpose in this moment.

Too many people think leadership is a responsibility that comes with a certain job title. But every single one of us has the ability, opportunity, and privilege to influence others, no matter our profession. In what areas of life do you influence people? How do your words and actions affect others?

_____

_____

_____

_____

_____

_____

_____

Affirmation Journal for Positive Thinking

Write your own leadership promise. As part of this promise, affirm what kind of leader you want to be, what you value, how you will impact the world, what you promise to deliver as a leader, who you will serve, and how you will do so.

_____

_____

_____

_____

_____

_____

_____

_____

_____

_____

_____

_____

EMBRACE POSITIVITY

Words powerfully reflect who we are and who we hope to become. These words take on even more power when wrapped in story, which makes what we say persuasive and motivating. Story gives words meaning. Story shows instead of tells. Story persuades where data cannot. As leaders, we can go one step further than just listing our values. We can tell our story.

This is the story of who we are, what we do, and *why* we do it—why the things we value mean so much to us. Every person has a story, and every story matters to the one who needs to hear it. If you don't have one already, craft the story of the leader you are and the leader you hope to become. We all have moments of leadership where we can impact another human being.

There is a time for everything, and I will patiently wait my turn, knowing that when it's time, it will happen.

My grandmother used to always say that patience is a virtue. A *virtue* is defined as a commendable trait or quality. Do you believe that patience is a virtue? If you had more patience, what might be different? Would having more of it help you in some aspect of your life?

_____

_____

_____

_____

_____

_____

_____

Affirmation Journal for Positive Thinking

Take a moment to consider that sometimes things happen how and when they do for a reason. Write out why it might be better for things NOT to happen as fast as you want them to. Create a positive affirmation to remind yourself that the universe has its own clock. _____

_____

_____

_____

_____

_____

_____

_____

_____

_____

_____

_____

EMBRACING POSITIVITY

Sometimes we get frustrated when life doesn't obey our schedule. Whether it's a relationship, partnership, career, achievement, having a family, or another opportunity, sometimes you find yourself wondering when it will be *your* turn. And then one day, it *is* your turn. And maybe a week later, it won't be.

When we're able to fully acknowledge that life runs on a different schedule than our plans, we are less anxious and more at peace. Often, we look back on those delayed opportunities and find that they actually happened at a much better time than we had planned. Maybe we were more prepared for what we wanted. Or perhaps that closed door led us to another one much better suited to us—maybe one we didn't even know existed. We enjoy life so much more when we can trust that it will be our turn—just maybe not today.

Today my most important job is to be fully present for those I love and those who love me.

Today's affirmation is about choosing to be fully present with those who matter most to you. Who are the ones you cherish? Make a list of these people or pets. What does it look like to be fully present in their lives? What does your presence bring to them and you?

Affirmation Journal for Positive Thinking

Take a moment to create a written promise to yourself. In this promise, make the vow to be fully present for the people who matter. Write down what that will look like. Talk about what this will mean to those who will receive more of your time and attention. _____

_____

_____

_____

_____

_____

_____

_____

_____

_____

_____

_____

_____

EMBRACE POSITIVITY

We all have our own definitions of what being present means (how it looks to us), just as we all have definitions of what love should look like. Here's the thing: Not all definitions match. For example, I might expect a friend to notice my new hairstyle as a sign that she is fully present with me, while in the same moment, my friend is waiting for me to notice that she wants to be invited inside to see my new house. In both instances, we are waiting for what we believe friendship should look like.

Be aware that attention is given and received in many ways. As you explore what "being present" looks like for you, consider that the receiver of your presence may have a different definition. Think about this: Is the point of being fully present to do it on your terms or someone else's?

Today I will release the weight of this burden I have been carrying around. It does not serve me.

We all carry burdens. Maybe for you it's a toxic relationship at home or at work. Maybe you're carrying the weight of something someone did to you. What burdens are you carrying around today? How are they impacting your life? What would it look like or feel like to release them?

Write a positive self-love statement about your burdens, focusing on how they might be serving you and how they are not. Remind yourself what you can control and what you can't. Affirm that you deserve your best life and that you do not have to keep carrying this weight around. _____

_____

_____

_____

_____

_____

_____

_____

_____

_____

_____

_____

_____

EMBRACE POSITIVITY

Before you can release a burden that doesn't serve you, you must identify the burden. This takes self-awareness, which is the first step to self-care. Remember, there is nothing selfish about making sure you are fully charged by first taking care of yourself.

Now write a letter to the burden you identified. Honor that it had a place in your life to teach you something and make you stronger. Then tell it that it's time to go because it no longer serves a purpose or holds a place in your thoughts. If this was a particularly heavy burden, you might want to treat its release with even more symbolism. For example, I like to write my burden down on a piece of paper and then burn the paper carefully in a fireplace or firepit.

Today I celebrate someone else's victory. Celebrating the success of others brings more of it into my own life.

How do you feel when someone else gets something you wanted, like that opportunity, that relationship, that reward, that job, or that promotion? How do you react? How do you treat them? How does their accomplishment make you feel about yourself? Do you feel like you lost or that it wasn't fair?

Affirmation Journal for Positive Thinking

Create an internal and external response that will help you react in a positive way when someone else gets what you wanted. Instead of focusing on bitter feelings, remind yourself that your turn is coming and that your happiness for others will bring more opportunities and happiness to you as a result. _____

_____

_____

_____

_____

_____

_____

_____

_____

_____

_____

_____

_____

EMBRACE POSITIVITY

Sometimes we may choose to feel that someone else's victory means our loss. That if they didn't choose us, it must mean there is something wrong with us. That if they win, we lose. But this is not always—and not even often—true. The next time someone gets the opportunity you wanted and you start to have negative thoughts, ask yourself if those thoughts are really true. Is there a chance that even a perceived loss can be reshaped into some sort of victory, lesson, or gift?

Whenever you feel tempted to react to someone else's win with bitterness, make the choice to feel something different. Choose to respond with words like, *"Well done! Congratulations for them. They deserved it. And I can't wait for the day I get an opportunity like that!"*

Today I joyfully play the role of artist, seeking creativity for its own sake and knowing that it produces my greatest ideas.

In what area of your life can you play the role of artist? Is it finding an old table and repainting it? Writing a song even though you've never done that before? Preparing a visually appealing meal? Brainstorm ways you can choose to be an artist just for the fun of it.

_____

_____

_____

_____

_____

_____

Think about the importance of creativity in your life and how being creative might help you in other areas. Create a positive statement that reminds you to seek creativity—to play like a child—with no rules or expected outcomes, just because you can. _____

_____

_____

_____

_____

_____

_____

_____

_____

_____

_____

_____

_____

EMBRACE POSITIVITY

Creativity isn't something only a few possess. Children have it in abundance. Life just tries to teach it out of us. We talk ourselves out of being creative because it feels frivolous and silly. But it isn't frivolous. Being creative sharpens our mind, increases our ability to be more innovative, and refreshes our spirit. And just because it feels silly doesn't make it true. We're just not all used to it, and we haven't seen the connection between the action and the result.

I believe that working our creativity muscle unlocks innovation in other areas. The simple act of journaling can tap into the most creative recesses of your soul. Often, I have rambled onto paper until suddenly a character pops up—or a story, a solution to a problem, or a business idea. The cool thing is that creation needs no outcome. You can create just for creation's sake. So go make something!

Today I will love someone who seems completely unlovable by making love a choice, not a feeling—not to serve them but to serve me.

Is someone in your life hard to love? Try to write a different story about that person that helps you love them anyway. Can you see their life from a different point of view? Has someone given you a second chance when you weren't acting very lovable?

Loving someone is a choice you can make; you don't need to hold on to resentment. Write an affirmation, your own manifesto, about how you will choose to love others—not for what it brings to them but for what it brings to you and why.

_____

_____

_____

_____

_____

_____

_____

_____

_____

_____

_____

_____

EMBRACE POSITIVITY

There may be days when the sight of someone makes you skip with joy and days when you want to run the other way. Most relationships start with a feeling of love—*we fell in love, we hit it off,* or *we felt a connection*—almost as if it was a coincidence. While that may often be how love starts, love lasts when that feeling becomes a choice: when we choose to love, even if we feel like running the other way.

One of the strongest motives I have for choosing love is knowing how often I am completely "unlovable." I can be incredibly annoying. When someone has the grace to love me anyway, it's a gift. When I focus on choosing love, it brings more love into my life. Who will you choose to love anyway to make the world a better place?

Before I speak, I ask myself, "Is this kind and does it serve?" If not, I let my silence speak instead.

How often do you engage in conversations that have gotten overly emotional? Do you always have an opinion? What about conversations that make you angry? Are you quick to respond? Are your words helping or hurting? What impact are your words having on those who hear them?

_____

_____

_____

_____

_____

_____

_____

Take a moment to create a policy for how you will respond during conversations, especially those that are emotionally heated. Think about the level of respect you want from your peers and what that looks like. Consider how your course of action reflects the way you want to be perceived. _____

_____

_____

_____

_____

_____

_____

_____

_____

_____

_____

_____

_____

EMBRACE POSITIVITY

Have you ever written an angry email or comment without sending/posting it, and then when you see it later, you feel shocked that you were actually going to say that? Me too. Emotional commenting can make us say things we don't really mean and can't take back. Sometimes I forget that my character is always on display. How I respond affects whether I am respected by those whose opinions matter to me.

Most situations aren't helped by a pileup of opinions. People aren't as impacted by *what* you say as much as *how* you say it. Sometimes silence is a sign of character, not of weakness, and the strongest action you can take is to do nothing. Once words are spoken or written, they're out there forever, so think about what you really want to say before you say it.

The universe is blessing me with abundance. I deserve this. I open my arms and rush in with joyful gratitude.

Are you pushing away your blessings because you think you don't deserve them? Do you think that wanting or having more money makes you selfish? Have you considered that the universe *wants* you to have this and that money is a sign that you are *serving* the world with your gifts?

List all your negative beliefs about money. Maybe you think you aren't worth
that much money, that it's bad to take money from others, or that it's honorable
to make do with less. Now cross out all these beliefs and list all the reasons why
money is a good thing; create an affirmation to solidify it. _____

_____

_____

_____

_____

_____

_____

_____

_____

_____

_____

_____

_____

EMBRACE POSITIVITY

Many successful people say that getting the fees you want starts with believing you deserve those fees. It's easier said than done. For some people, it takes reprogramming their inner script: replacing the negative belief with the positive one, repeating the new belief over and over, and then acting on it.

Stand in front of a mirror and practice telling yourself that you are worth it and deserve it. Tell yourself that it's just money; it's not emotional. When you start truly believing money is just currency, you will stop attaching feelings to your fee. Don't assume that people don't want to bless you for your gift. Sometimes it's as simple as the fact that they have a certain amount to spend and your service has a certain price. Learn to see the value in your gift for the receiver. You will often find you're not charging them enough.

I am loved beyond measure. And because of that, today I return that love to others, which helps make the world a better place.

We attract what we put into the world, so acts of kindness will serve us in return. Sometimes we are so busy that we forget to do this. Where can you bring a little unexpected happiness into someone else's life? How will you find those opportunities?

_____

_____

_____

_____

_____

_____

_____

Look at all the different times during your day when you have the opportunity to do something kind and unexpected for a stranger or a friend. Create an affirmation or a series of affirmations:

When I go to _____

_____

_____

_____

and see _____

_____,

I will _____

_____

_____

_____

_____

_____

to make their day brighter.

EMBRACE POSITIVITY

When someone shows you unexpected kindness, it becomes a special memory—a gift that never leaves you, making it worth far more than its initial monetary value. It's the person in line ahead of you who paid for your coffee, the nurse who held your hand and took a moment to sit with you, or the teacher who noticed you needed clothes and found a way to get them for you.

Consider creating a "random acts of kindness" notebook and schedule a weekly plan to do something kind for somebody. Put it on your calendar like any other commitment. Document what happens and how it makes you feel. It will be fun to watch kindness enter your own life in unexpected ways, because that's how it works. Share your project with others, and challenge them to join the movement. Imagine how our world would change if everybody did something like this.

Today I breathe through my anxiety and focus on gratitude, knowing that it will ground me and bring me peace.

Is there something creating anxiety in your life right now? Inside your house? Within your family? In your community? In your state or country? If you had to name your fear, what would it be? Is there a deeper fear underneath? Take a moment to state your worries.

_____

_____

_____

_____

_____

_____

_____

Affirmation Journal for Positive Thinking

Now that you've honored your feelings, shift your focus from what you cannot control to what you can, from what you don't have to what you do, and from what isn't happening to what is. With this in mind, create a positive statement you can turn to for comfort when worry enters your mind. _____

_____

_____

_____

_____

_____

_____

_____

_____

_____

_____

_____

EMBRACE POSITIVITY

Worry doesn't serve us or solve our problems. It impacts our health and happiness, and it steers us down a dark road. That's why so many experts point to the positive impact of a gratitude list. Yes, we've heard it before, because it's a time-tested truth: Focusing on the good—what we're grateful for—is how we release anxiety and worry.

When we program our brain with love, peace, joy, happiness, and gratitude, our body, mind, and spirit obey and steer us down the path of light. In times of great sorrow and struggle, we often have to dig really deep to find what grounds us. Maybe you're not sure, and that's totally okay. Maybe today is the day you set out to find it. Joy doesn't just live at the destination; it waits for you at the next step. Today is a great day to breathe and start your gratitude list.

I will not give up. I will play hard and keep fighting until the last whistle blows.

Are you running out of steam? Do you feel like giving up? Where are you losing energy in your life? Maybe it's a dream that feels like it's taking forever. Or maybe you're a caregiver and you're very tired. Or maybe you are physically out of gas. Where are your fuel tanks running low?

_____

_____

_____

_____

_____

_____

_____

Affirmation Journal for Positive Thinking

What you tell yourself in moments when you feel like you have no more to give is critical. This is when you need to become your own cheerleader and coach. What do you need to hear from your supporters to keep going? Write it down and say it to yourself often. _____

_____

_____

_____

_____

_____

_____

_____

_____

_____

_____

_____

_____

EMBRACE POSITIVITY

I often think about how many athletes were trained by their coaches to fight until the last whistle of the game. I actually made that one of my affirmations to help me when I feel like I'm in danger of quitting. We all have moments where we get weary, when it feels like we're never going to get to where we are going.

So today I remind you that the game isn't over until the last whistle blows. You are not out. You don't quit. You can do this. I believe in you. Now I want you to believe in yourself, too. Need a reminder? Go watch that movie that always makes you cheer at the end. Works for me! Now get back in the game. That last whistle hasn't blown yet.

Today I define exactly how victory looks and feels in my life. I claim it as my own. I've already won.

What does winning look like to you? Describe your victory. Include every juicy detail. What are the sounds, the feelings, the smells? Rate the intensity. What does it bring into your life? Paint a clear picture for yourself—and don't be afraid to dream really big!

Affirmation Journal for Positive Thinking

Create your own victory moment in a creative way. Maybe you'll film a short video or make a flip-book with words and pictures. Perhaps you'll write a song or paint a picture. It doesn't matter what you do as long as you can see it in vivid color. Write a positive affirmation that describes your victory moment.

_____

_____

_____

_____

_____

_____

_____

_____

_____

_____

_____

EMBRACE POSITIVITY

I once asked a professional athlete, "What separates the ones who make it and the ones who don't?" He immediately answered, "The ones who win walk onto that course already knowing that they won." If you ask coaches in other sports, they would agree that your mindset when you step onto that field is critical. Maybe it isn't enough to win, but without it, you are guaranteed failure. My philosophy is the same in life.

If you go into a project wondering, worrying, afraid, and convinced you won't be able to achieve it, then you have already sabotaged it. When you think you can't, you are working against yourself and your brain and body start to obey. Affirmations are important because you teach yourself to aim for victory instead of failure.

Today I focus on my legacy: the footprint I leave on this world. I will align my current self with my future self.

If you were to look way ahead to the final days of your life, what do you think will matter then? What will you want people to say about you? What evidence of your time here on this earth do you want to exist and why?

_____

_____

_____

_____

_____

_____

_____

_____

Affirmation Journal for Positive Thinking

Create a positive reminder as a routine check-in on what really matters in your life from the perspective of your future self. See if your life matches up with where you want to go. Make sure your top priorities are really getting your undivided attention. Affirm what really matters. _____

_____

_____

_____

_____

_____

_____

_____

_____

_____

_____

_____

_____

_____

EMBRACE POSITIVITY

I've worked with companies that spend a lot of energy trying to make their customers and employees happy, and it never seems to work. That's because they are focusing on the wrong goal. It's not about making people happy; it's about making them feel valued. I believe most people at their core want to know that they matter—that they make a difference.

As we grow older, we find that many of the things we thought mattered really didn't. If we look at life through the lens of our future, we can often see today more clearly. I wrote my own eulogy once and found that I was living my life out of balance. The things that meant most to me were getting the least attention. Understanding what *you* value and why it matters and aligning yourself with that brings peace.

With only so many minutes and so many things that can be done, I will guard my time as precious and cherish my moments.

How much of your day is spent dealing with other people's problems? How often does your schedule get disrupted by something you didn't plan for? How many of your priorities are set aside because of someone else's? How is this impacting your life? Are your priorities being ignored?

_____

_____

_____

_____

_____

_____

Affirmation Journal for Positive Thinking

Write a positive statement that defines how you will take control of your time, how you will say no without guilt, and why you're doing this. Describe how your priorities are affected if you ignore them for someone else's wants. Read this statement whenever you are tempted to break your own rule._____

_____

_____

_____

_____

_____

_____

_____

_____

_____

_____

_____

_____

EMBRACE POSITIVITY

Most of us have more to do than time to do it. Have you ever planned your daily schedule to allow for some "you" time, and suddenly you get an email and another one and a phone call and something else that disrupts your plan? It can create a lot of stress, not to mention loss of that "you" time you really needed.

Time is precious. Often, we either don't value it as much as we should, or we operate as if there is an unlimited amount of it. The truth is that when you say yes to something, you say no to something else. Often someone else's issue takes you away from what you value most. This is not okay. Sure, sometimes you don't have a choice, but many times, you do. Honor your priorities. Plan, respect the plan, and don't feel guilty about saying no.

Today I will be a source of joy to people and bring a radiant burst of energy to every room.

It may feel silly to be silly, but why not give it a try? Can you do something to make someone laugh today? How can you be a source of humor and levity? What is the positive result of bringing joy into a room? What does silly look like on you?

What if you created your own joy handbook or humor manifesto? That's right: a job description for your day or moment of silliness—not just a guidebook on what to do, but why it matters. Write an affirmation about the positive impact you would have in your world. _____

_____

_____

_____

_____

_____

_____

_____

_____

_____

_____

_____

_____

EMBRACE POSITIVITY

There are quite a few studies showing a positive correlation between happiness and productivity in the workforce. There are even more studies that show how much an employee's happiness factors into their decision to stay at or leave a job. In my work, I have come to the simple conclusion that life is short, being happy is better than being angry, and happiness is contagious. I have also seen that making people happy makes me happy, too.

It is amazing how the joyful spirit of someone in a room can impact everyone there. That's enough for me to invite more of it into my life. Let's join all of those who are able to find the humor in every day! I don't think I've ever heard anybody complain about having too much joy. Don't worry that it might keep you from getting the work done; studies have proven just the opposite.

I choose my feelings; they don't choose me. Yes, I *can* help how I feel. I hold the power.

Is there a negative emotion you've been holding on to for a while? Tell me about it. Do you ever find yourself saying, "But I can't help how I feel"? Is that really true? Are you helpless in feeling that way, or can you choose to feel something different?

Affirmation Journal for Positive Thinking

Create a positive statement that guides you to choose how you will feel and therefore how you will react to an unpleasant situation. This affirmation will give you a chance to remind yourself that *you* choose your feelings; the feelings don't choose you._____

_____

_____

_____

_____

_____

_____

_____

_____

_____

_____

_____

EMBRACE POSITIVITY

When I was younger and faced challenging situations, I didn't really know how to deal with my negative emotions. I had been taught to stop crying and move on; get over it. As I grew older, I realized that it is perfectly okay to have emotions and to feel them. It doesn't make me weak; it makes me human. But then I would find myself rolling around in that emotion until it was controlling me. I just couldn't let it go. I would justify that by saying, "I can't help how I feel."

Then I learned that there comes a moment in that specific journey where I do get to make a choice: to choose happy or sad, angry or grateful, anxious or peaceful. I *can* help how I feel. What freedom this has brought me! Life is always better when you choose your feelings instead of letting them choose you.

Today I fill up my love bank, knowing that with every deposit I make, I am storing up riches.

Where are you making love deposits? How are you showing appreciation to others in your world? What does that look like? Could you do more? Kind words? An anonymous good deed? A love note dropped into someone's bag? List what you can do and who you can do it for.

Affirmation Journal for Positive Thinking

Set aside time in your calendar or on your to-do list to intentionally love on someone in a measurable way. When you get to this appointment or reach this item on your list, make it a priority just like you would paying your bills. Create an affirmation about how you fill your love bank. _____

_____

_____

_____

_____

_____

_____

_____

_____

_____

_____

_____

EMBRACE POSITIVITY

Try this exercise with a roommate, colleague, loved one, or family member: Put a clean jar in a common area. Each day (or each week), write something you love or appreciate about the other person on a strip of paper and place it in the jar. Plan a time to review the contents together.

This activity will have a positive impact on your relationship, and it will keep you and the other person in a constant state of looking for the good in others. It will also feel great to hear how much you're appreciated. We often don't hear that enough. Oh, and by the way, I am thankful that you are reading this book. It means a lot to me that you invested in my dream. I appreciate you. See how it works? Just dropped another penny in my bank.

I am meant for great things. I am here for a mighty purpose. I was created for a reason. Even if I have trouble seeing it, it is true.

Why do you think you're here? Look at the evidence in your life of times when you were there for someone else. What else have you brought into this world? No matter how small you think it seems, list it anyway. Think about the ripple effect of these things you've done.

_____

_____

_____

_____

_____

_____

Imagine there's someone across from you who feels worthless—who doesn't think anybody would miss them if they were gone, who thinks they just don't matter to the world. What would you tell them? Take time crafting your answer. Done? Now go read it to yourself. That letter is for you, too. _____

_____

_____

_____

_____

_____

_____

_____

_____

_____

_____

_____

EMBRACE POSITIVITY

Many would agree that our existence here is intentional. Our steps lead us to places where we have the opportunity and power to do something good. I think most big things in life are really a culmination of small things. Just as the body depends on every single part, life depends on every single person. You are cherished, valued, and here on purpose—for a purpose.

While our view is limited and we will never be able to see life from every perspective, we can still trust that the steps we take impact us all. You are here for a reason. You have a mighty purpose. Your life matters—even if today you can't see it. I believe in you. Now it's time for you to believe in yourself. And please know that today's message was given to you on purpose, not by accident.

Today I pay close attention to the words I say to others and who else may be listening.

How do your words come across? You might be a great communicator and get the job done, but how are your words actually landing? If you don't know, how can you find out? Is there a chance that your words are drowning out your intentions?

Spend some time today thinking about someone you know who is hurtful with their words. Now think about someone whose words are always comforting and kind, even when they are not saying something you want to hear. Affirm how you want your words to come across and how you will make that happen.

_____

_____

_____

_____

_____

_____

_____

_____

_____

_____

_____

EMBRACE POSITIVITY

Good communication skills are important. But sometimes we're so focused on what needs to be said that we aren't paying attention to how we are saying it and how it is being received. While your intention may be kind, that doesn't mean your words are.

Author of *The Healing Code*, Dr. Alex Loyd, really opened my eyes to how much we are affected by the words we hear. In his book, he gives one example of an adult who was greatly impacted by something her mother said to her when she was little. As it turns out, the statement wasn't even negative on the surface, but the child processed it in a negative light. That one small statement had affected her in a major way. We certainly can't control how someone processes what we say, but we can take a closer look at the words we use. Not sure how your words are landing? Why not ask?

My life will not change until I am willing to do the necessary work. Information means nothing without action.

Have you ever bought a book you didn't read? A treadmill that now holds clothes in the basement? What about a business planner that became out-of-date before you wrote anything in it? Me too. What do you think makes you follow through on some things and not others?

_____

_____

_____

_____

_____

_____

_____

Affirmation Journal for Positive Thinking

Think of one project you have been putting off. Come up with a list of *new* compelling reasons to follow through with it. The goal is to tap into what will really motivate you to complete the project. Now write a positive, motivating affirmation to help you get the job done. _____

_____

_____

_____

_____

_____

_____

_____

_____

_____

_____

_____

_____

EMBRACE POSITIVITY

I am the queen of getting excited about an idea and not following through. Luckily, I've learned to manage this trait, so I don't have a life of uncompleted projects. How? By finding a better why. For example, I knew I needed to exercise because everybody else was doing it. I knew it was important because, well, it just is. WRONG. No wonder I found every excuse not to exercise. I hadn't tied it to something I really wanted. I needed to find a better why.

Life really does give you all the answers you need—*if* you are willing to do the work. If not, either be honest with yourself and move on, or find a better why. Not one single thing in this journal will be effective if you don't put in the work. Not one. Information is useless without action. Go find a better why.

My dream is precious. It deserves the best people to support it. I will intentionally choose those who will support my dream.

Who are the people in your corner? Who has your back? Who have you chosen to surround yourself with? Are you carrying your burden alone? Are you reaching out to the people who can help? Do the people you trust with your dream lift you up or bring you down?

Affirmation Journal for Positive Thinking

Write a promise to yourself about your dream team. What will it look like?

Whether your team is friendship, volunteer, or paid, clarify how it supports you.

And just as important, define your boundaries with those who don't support it.

How will you gracefully deflect them? _____

_____

_____

_____

_____

_____

_____

_____

_____

_____

_____

_____

_____

EMBRACE POSITIVITY

My wish is for you to have an amazing dream team like mine, made up of people whose opinions matter and who lovingly support you: people who are cheerleaders, fans of your work, and strong enough to guide you and keep you accountable. I admire people who don't just tell me what I *want* to hear, but what I *need* to hear.

Let's value the sanctity of that space we give to our dream team by having strict guidelines. It has taken me years (and some big mistakes) to learn how I want my dream team to operate. The people you surround yourself with are too important to this dream to leave to chance. There can and will be plenty of people who play a part in your life, but be selective about who is on your dream team and know how to define the boundaries between the two.

Today I will have that tough conversation. I will be firm but kind and say what needs to be said.

Is there a conversation you need to have that you have been putting off? How will *not* having this conversation impact your life? If you did have this conversation, how would things change? What would happen? How can you approach this?

_____

_____

_____

_____

_____

_____

_____

Affirmation Journal for Positive Thinking

Make a written commitment to yourself to have this necessary conversation. Plan what you'll say so that you don't speak in haste, out of anger, or in a way that creates conflict or confusion. Come from the perspective of "I feel" instead of "you always." Give the other person space to reflect and respond.

_____

_____

_____

_____

_____

_____

_____

_____

_____

_____

_____

_____

_____

EMBRACE POSITIVITY

Sometimes we delay that tough conversation even though we know the situation will just get worse. We might be afraid to hurt someone's feelings, of how they may retaliate, or that we'll lose a friend. Sometimes we may not be willing to accept the consequences. Maybe we know that saying these words will end the relationship or the job or cause a rift.

That's why it's important to clarify the real issue and what you expect the other person to do as a result. Don't discuss people; discuss an issue that needs to be solved. Conversations that simply place blame don't take you to a better place. Sometimes you must ask whether a conversation is really necessary. We have many opportunities in life to forgive someone's behavior for the sake of a greater good. Sometimes the consequences really aren't worth the conversation. Only you can be the judge.

Today I will learn someone else's love language to treat them in the way they personally define love.

What is your love language? In other words, how do you like to receive love? Kind words? Gestures? Gifts or cards? Invitations to spend time? Now think about someone you care about. How does that person show you they care? Do you each have a different love language?

_____

_____

_____

_____

_____

_____

_____

_____

Affirmation Journal for Positive Thinking

List some people who are important to you. Think about how they might like to feel valued and appreciated. Create a positive affirmation that will help you determine how others like to receive love (instead of how *you* define it), and act on it. _____

_____

_____

_____

_____

_____

_____

_____

_____

_____

_____

_____

EMBRACE POSITIVITY

Dr. Gary Chapman, author of *The 5 Love Languages*, was the first to popularize the concept that people want to receive love in different ways. This was eye-opening for me, as I had just assumed I was supposed to treat others the way I wanted to be treated. As it turns out, that's not always the case.

While I might be upset that a friend didn't call me on a special day, that friend might show me she cares by doing thoughtful things for me on other days of the year. I might call my friend on her special days, but she might be upset that I didn't come to her child's play. We would both be looking for the same thing in different places. There are many things we do to show others we care for them, but it never hurts to occasionally step back and look at how *they* care for others. It's a pretty good sign of what they would like in return.

Today I look in the mirror, beyond my outer appearance to my inner strength, and admire my character.

What about your character are you most proud of? What are the values that guide your life? How are they reflected in what you do, what you say, and how you treat people? What priority do you place on your character? What do you want others to say about you?

Affirmation Journal for Positive Thinking

Create a detailed list of positive statements about your character. Sell the strengths of who you are with the same passion you would sell something you are really excited about. Explain what good character brings into the world. Write down the positive impact you have on your community. _____

_____

_____

_____

_____

_____

_____

_____

_____

_____

_____

_____

_____

EMBRACE POSITIVITY

Sometimes the world makes us believe that our worth is tied up in how we look, how strong we are, where we live, what we drive, or the things we've achieved and acquired. But being loved for how much you have is very empty. Being worthy because of the way your face looks is not going to last. The people who care the most about us probably don't care that we have achieved something they haven't—and, if they do, then perhaps that's not going to last, either.

Our character is the thing that outlives us. That isn't dependent on how we look in the mirror, and it can't be taken away by someone else. I don't know about you, but I think that's pretty amazing. So go admire your character. And if it needs a little work, don't worry. We all do. And it's never too late to change.

Today I honor that not everyone will stay in my life forever. I will be okay with letting go.

Are you hanging on to a relationship that no longer serves you? Do you believe that friends are forever? Are you blaming yourself because your team fell apart or an employee quit? Do you have unrealistic ideas of how long a relationship, friendship, or partnership should last?

Affirmation Journal for Positive Thinking

Create a positive affirmation giving yourself permission to let a relationship go. Honor that the person served an important purpose in your life, and then release yourself of anger, burden, or blame. Respect that life has different seasons and people often come and go—and that's okay._____

_____

_____

_____

_____

_____

_____

_____

_____

_____

_____

_____

EMBRACE POSITIVITY

Sometimes we expect so much of others that we take it personally when they leave our circle. We harbor a grudge over a friend who used to be close and now never calls. We may feel guilt that we hired someone who didn't work out. Or we may be angry that a close coworker decided to work somewhere else. What other people do is beyond our control. Just because they moved into a different life phase is no reason to think any less of the time you had together.

Life is filled with seasons of growth, and we become different versions of ourselves. These changes bring new relationships and sometimes end old ones. Just because someone stopped calling doesn't mean they don't like you. It could just mean they're in a different season of their life, and the door is opening for you to welcome in the person who's just been sent to yours.

Resources

BOOKS

The 7 Habits of Highly Effective People, 4th Edition, by Stephen R. Covey (Simon & Schuster, 2020)

Who Hijacked My Fairy Tale? by Kelly Swanson (Independently Published, 2009)

PODCASTS

The Good Life Project Podcast: GoodLifeProject.com/podcast

Tony Robbins Podcast: TonyRobbins.com/podcasts

MOTIVATIONAL & INSPIRATIONAL VIDEOS

Goalcast: YouTube.com/channel/UCc4IYtPKkJLSAHHuJx1GiGQ

References

Arnold, Linda. "75-Year Harvard Study: What Makes Us Happy?" *AP News*. April 21, 2019. APNews.com/article/6dab1e79c34e4514af8d184d951f5733.

Chapman, Gary. *The 5 Love Languages: The Secret to Love that Lasts.* Chicago: Northfield Publishing, 2015.

Loyd, Alexander, and Ben Johnson. *The Healing Code: 6 Minutes to Heal the Source of Your Health, Success, or Relationship Issue*. New York: Grand Central Life & Style, 2013.

Mineo, Liz. "Good Genes Are Nice, but Joy Is Better." *The Harvard Gazette*. April 11, 2017. News.Harvard.edu/gazette/story/2017/04/over-nearly-80-years-harvard -study-has-been-showing-how-to-live-a-healthy-and-happy-life.

University of Oxford. "Happy Workers Are 13% More Productive." *University of Oxford News & Events*. October 24, 2019. OX.AC.uk/news/2019-10-24-happy -workers-are-13-more-productive.

University of Warwick. "New Study Shows We Work Harder When We Are Happy." Warwick News & Events. Updated October 18, 2021. Warwick.AC.uk /newsandevents/pressreleases/new_study_shows.

About the Author

Kelly Swanson is an award-winning storyteller, motivational speaker, comedian, and strategic storytelling expert. She was a cast member of *The Fashion Hero* TV show, a featured entertainer for Holland America Line cruises, and a contributor to *The Huffington Post*. She is the author of *The Story Formula* and *Who Hijacked My Fairy Tale?*

Kelly launched her one-woman theater production, *Who Hijacked My Fairy Tale?*, in January 2020. She is also the creator of an online story series called *Prides Hollow, the small town with a big heart*. People all over the world have been inspired and charmed by Kelly's programs. She lives with her family in North Carolina. For more about Kelly, visit MotivationalSpeakerKellySwanson.com.

CPSIA information can be obtained
at www.ICGtesting.com
Printed in the USA
BVHW020912130122
626142BV00014B/349